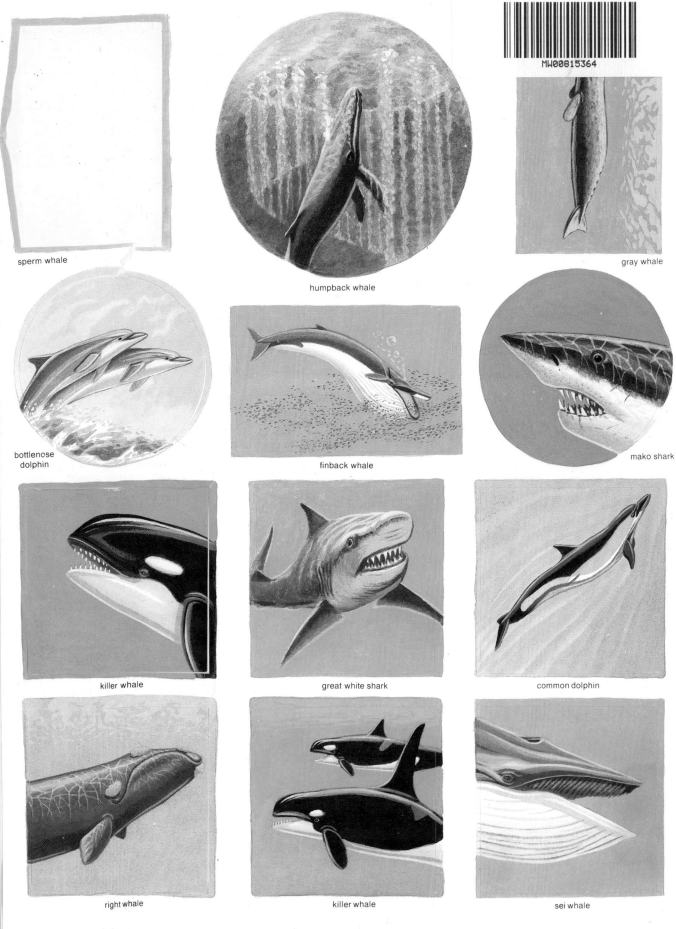

sperm whale

humpback whale

gray whale

bottlenose dolphin

finback whale

mako shark

killer whale

great white shark

common dolphin

right whale

killer whale

sei whale

Plate 1

minke whale

great white shark

hammerhead shark

basking shark

false killer whale

whale shark

spectacled porpoise

humpback whale

bottlenose dolphin

wobbegong

tiger shark

thresher shark

Plate 2

leopard shark

humpback whale

blue shark

gray whale

gray nurse shark

beluga

narwhal

Amazon River dolphin

goblin shark

rough-tooth dolphin

whitetip shark

bowhead whale

Plate 3